THE GREAT ARTISTS
Michelangelo

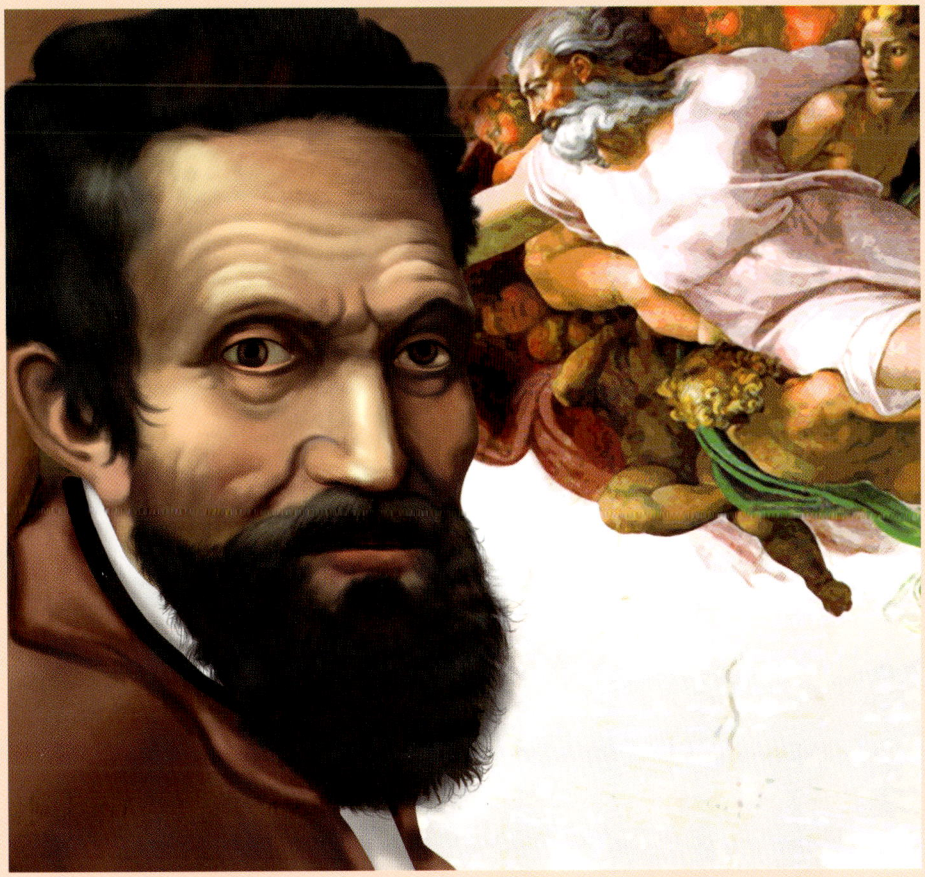

Om KIDZ
An imprint of Om Books International

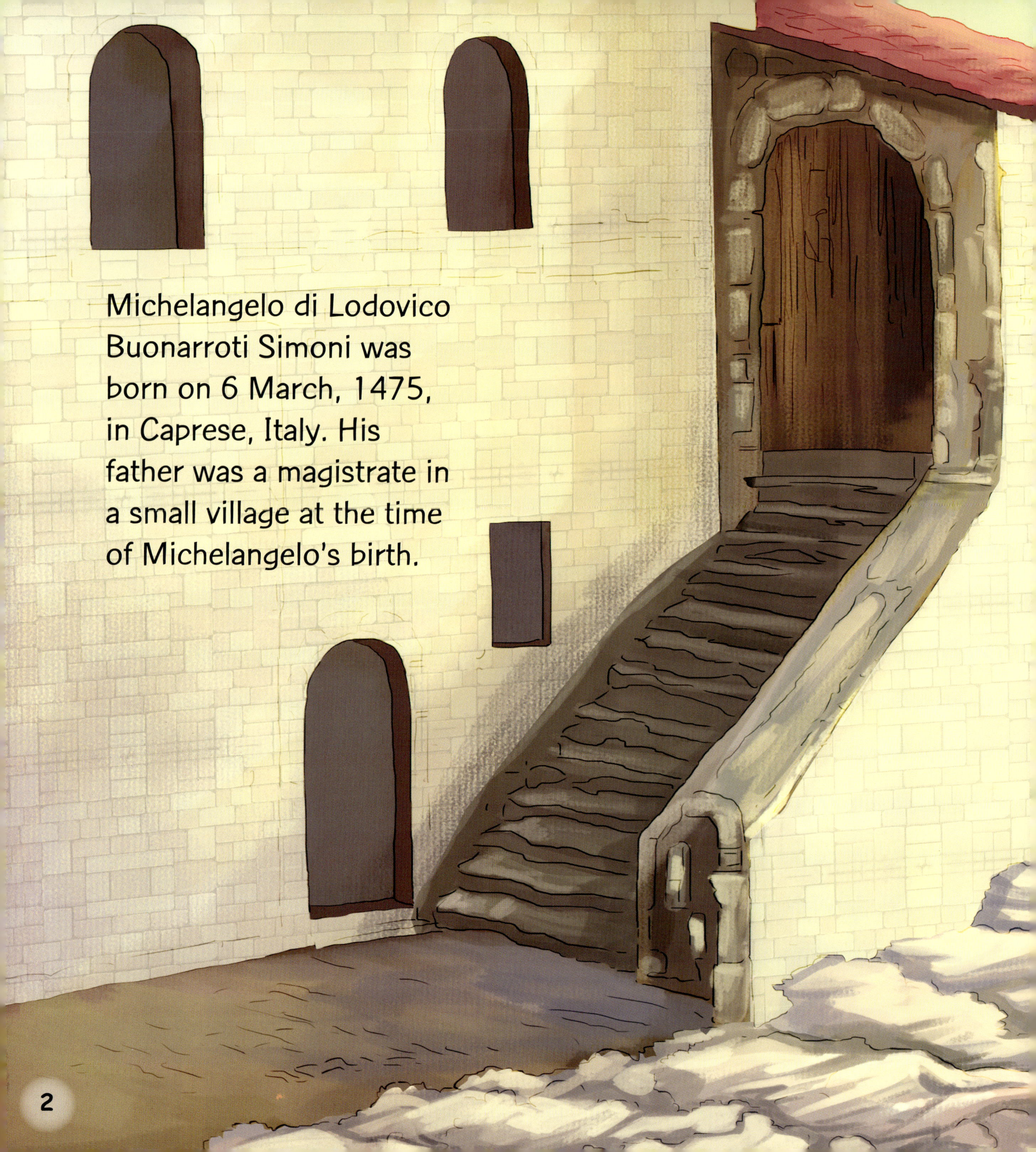

Michelangelo di Lodovico Buonarroti Simoni was born on 6 March, 1475, in Caprese, Italy. His father was a magistrate in a small village at the time of Michelangelo's birth.

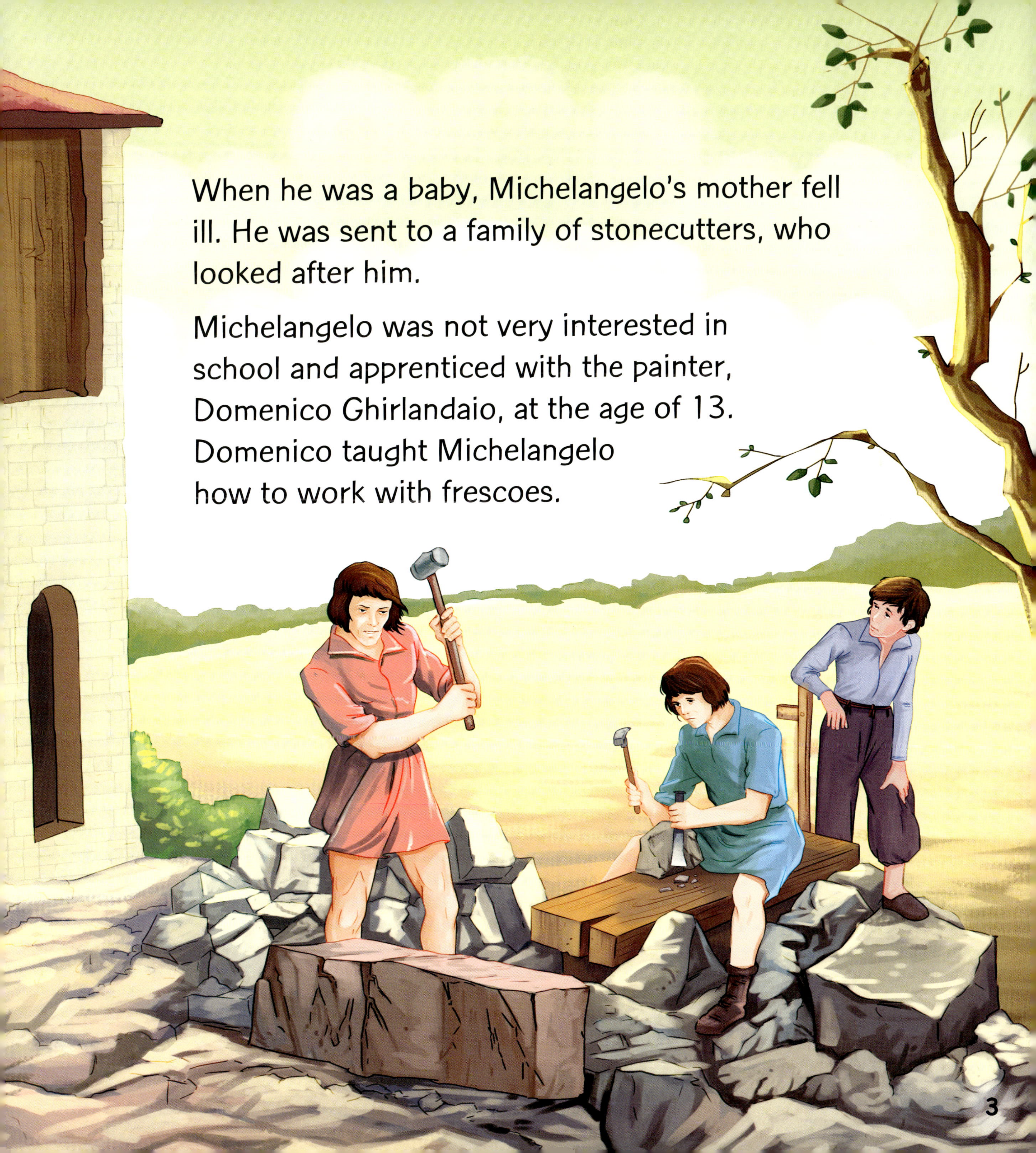

When he was a baby, Michelangelo's mother fell ill. He was sent to a family of stonecutters, who looked after him.

Michelangelo was not very interested in school and apprenticed with the painter, Domenico Ghirlandaio, at the age of 13. Domenico taught Michelangelo how to work with frescoes.

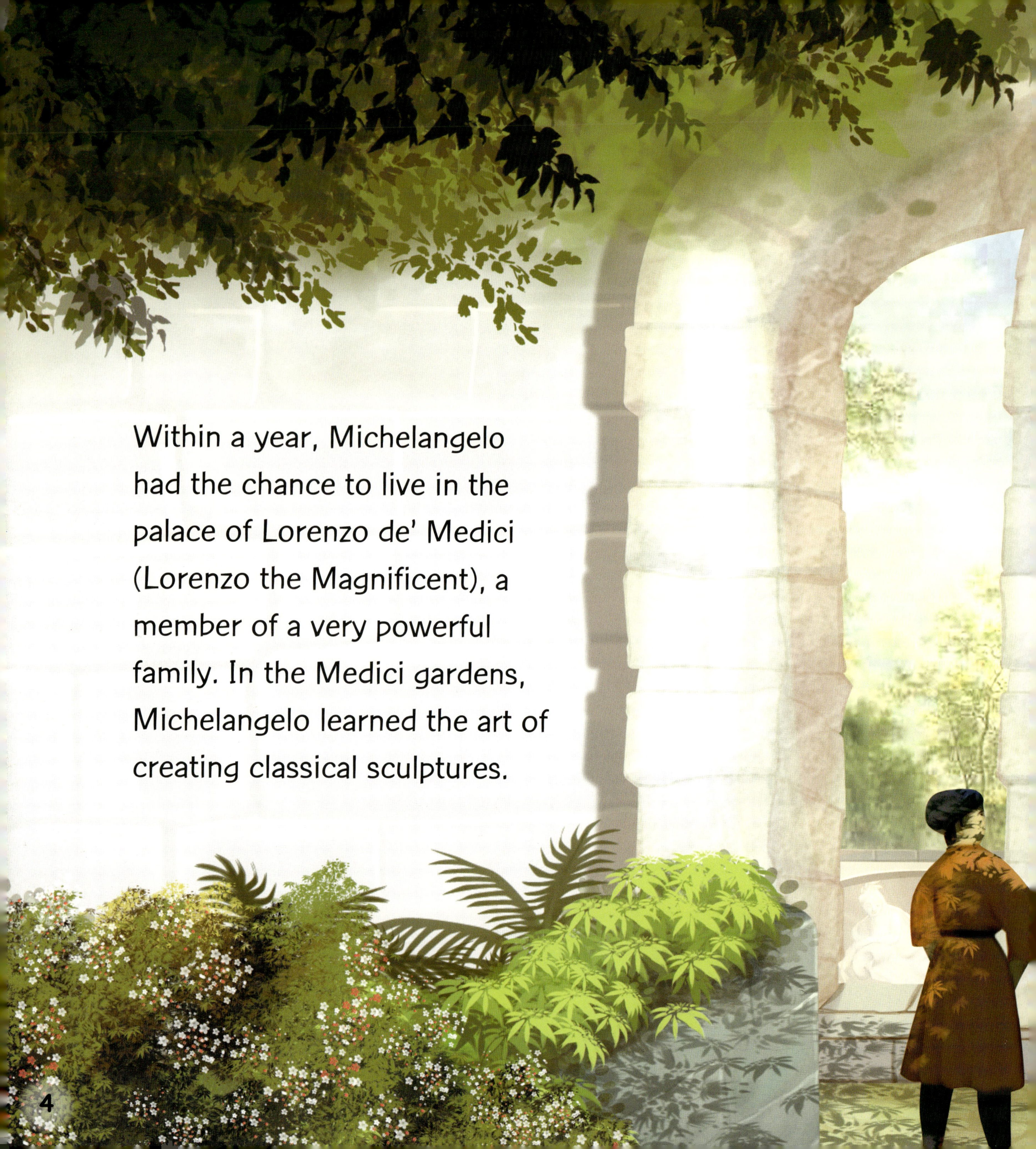

Within a year, Michelangelo had the chance to live in the palace of Lorenzo de' Medici (Lorenzo the Magnificent), a member of a very powerful family. In the Medici gardens, Michelangelo learned the art of creating classical sculptures.

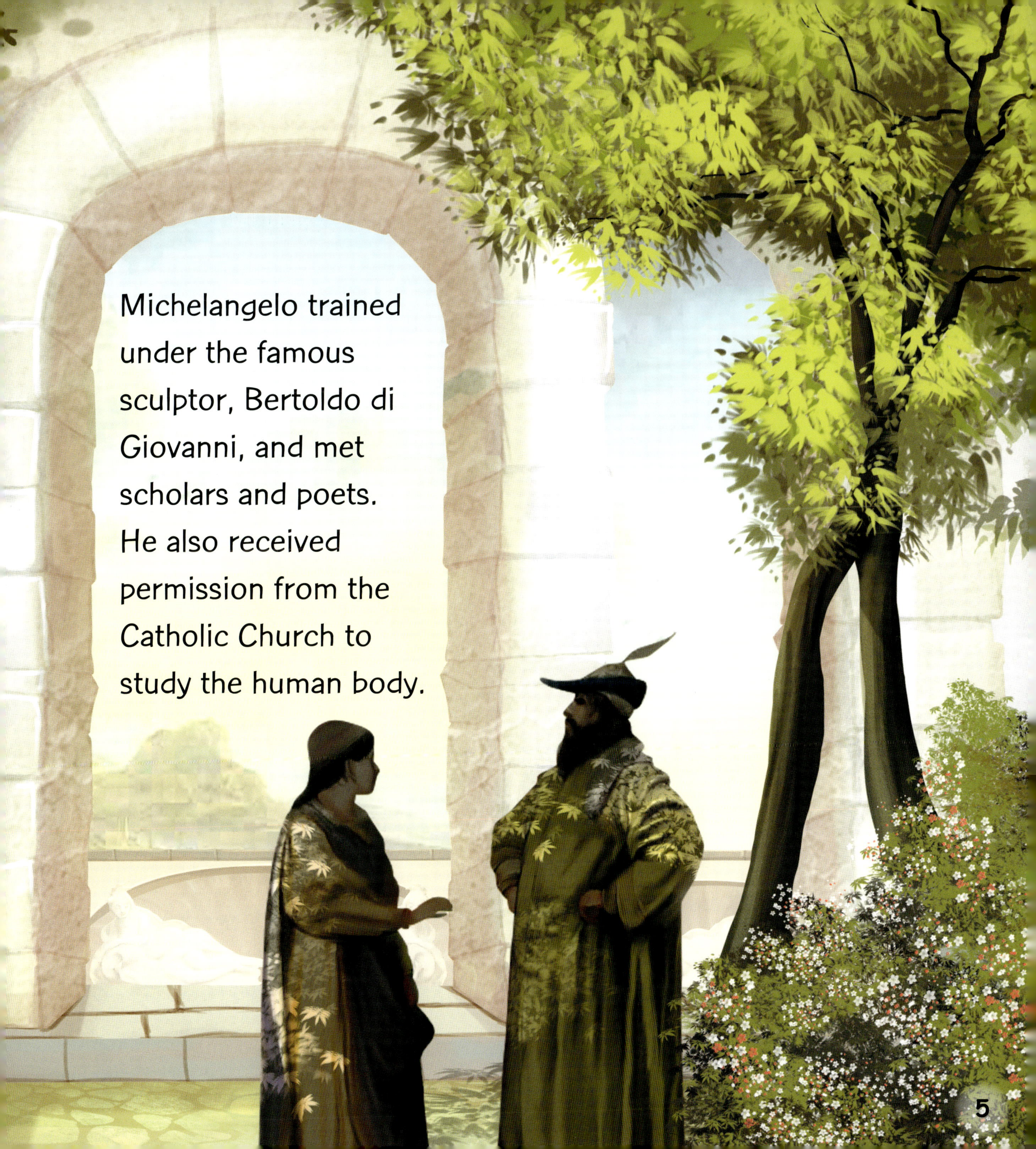

Michelangelo trained under the famous sculptor, Bertoldo di Giovanni, and met scholars and poets. He also received permission from the Catholic Church to study the human body.

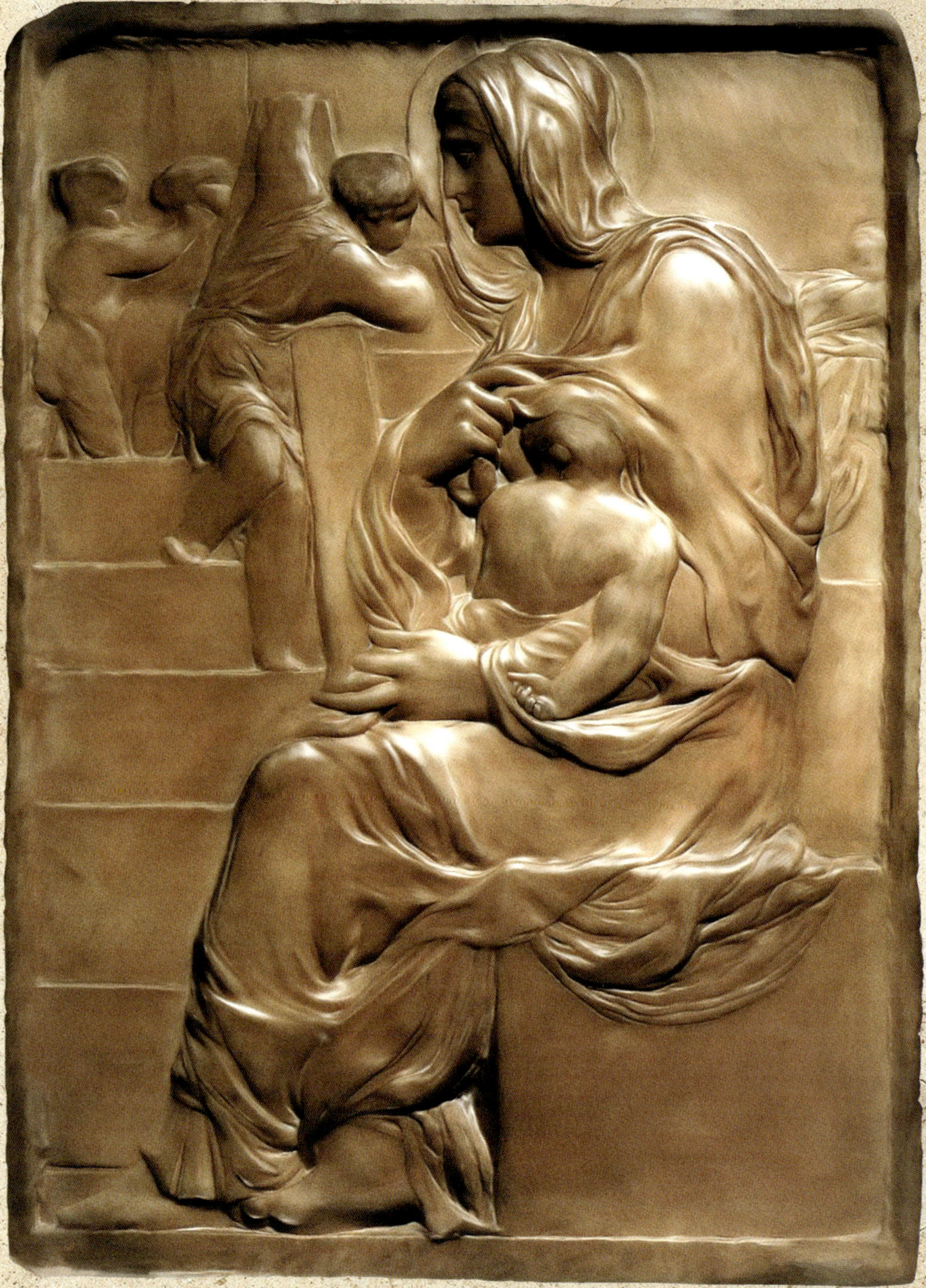

When Michelangelo moved to Rome, he created *The Pieta*. This sculpture showed Mary holding Jesus on her lap after his crucifixion. It was made from a single block of marble and was completed in a year. Michelangelo was only 25 years old at the time.

According to legend, Michelangelo heard some pilgrims say that another artist had created *The Pieta*. To prove it was his work, Michelangelo signed his name on the sash in front of Mary's dress. It is the only sculpture to bear his signature.

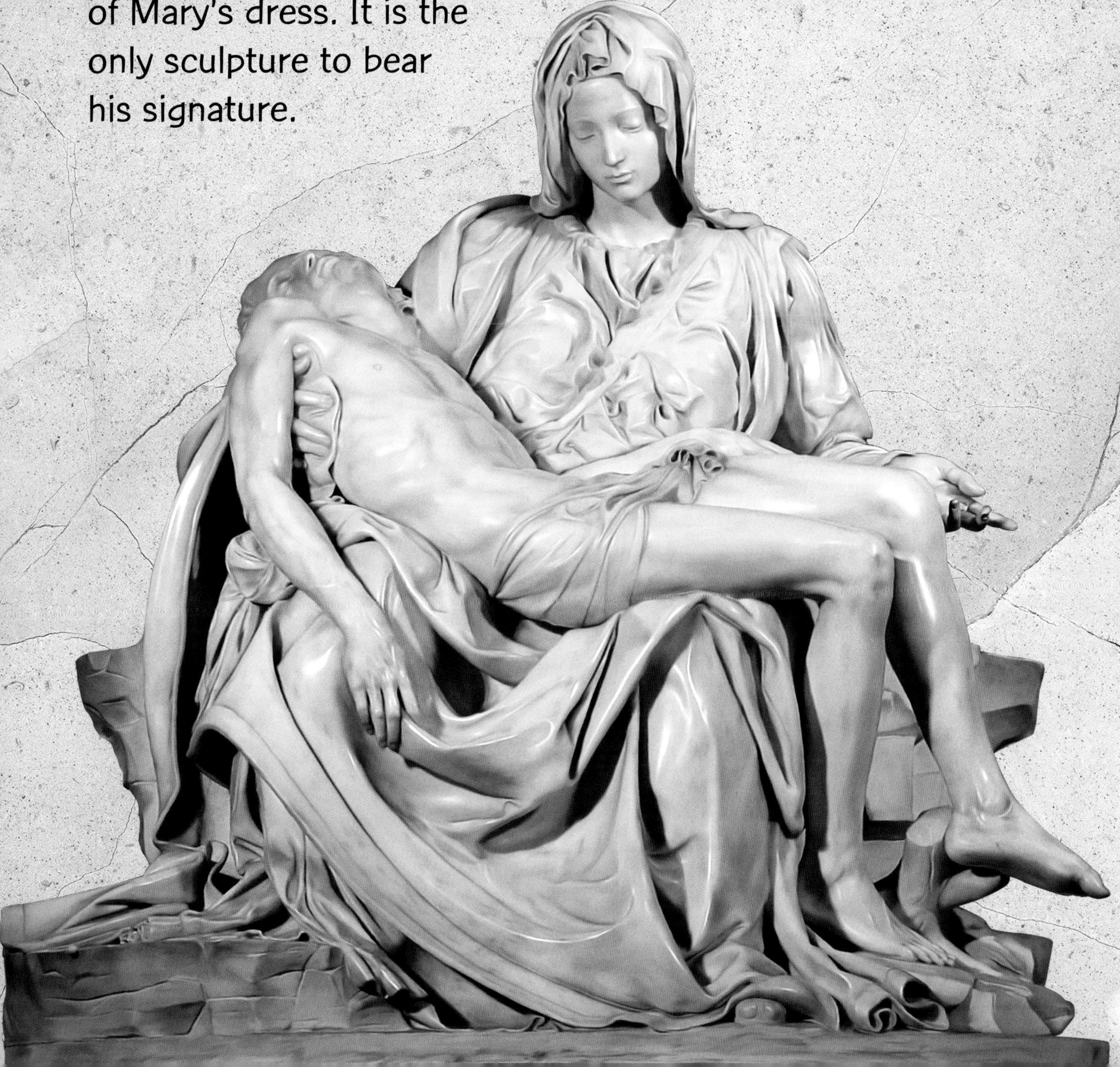

Michelangelo accepted a commission to create *David*, which had already been abandoned by two sculptors. He transformed a huge narrow slab or marble into the impressive figure of *David*. It is considered to be the most perfect sculpture of all time.

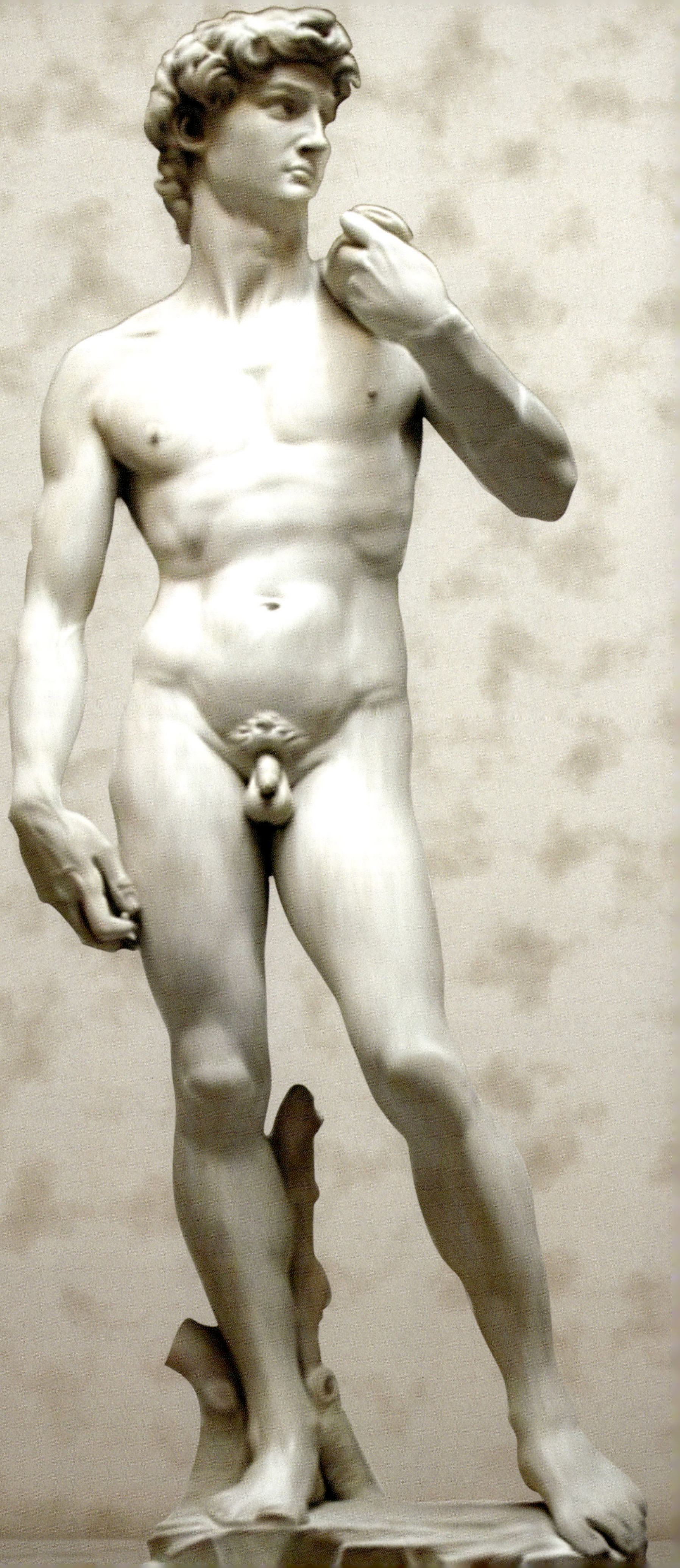

Pope Julius II commissioned Michelangelo to decorate the ceiling of the Sistine Chapel. This fuelled Michelangelo's imagination and he used the ceiling as a canvas for paintings that featured over 300 characters. However, the work had to be taken down soon after completion due to a fungal infection in the plaster of the ceiling.

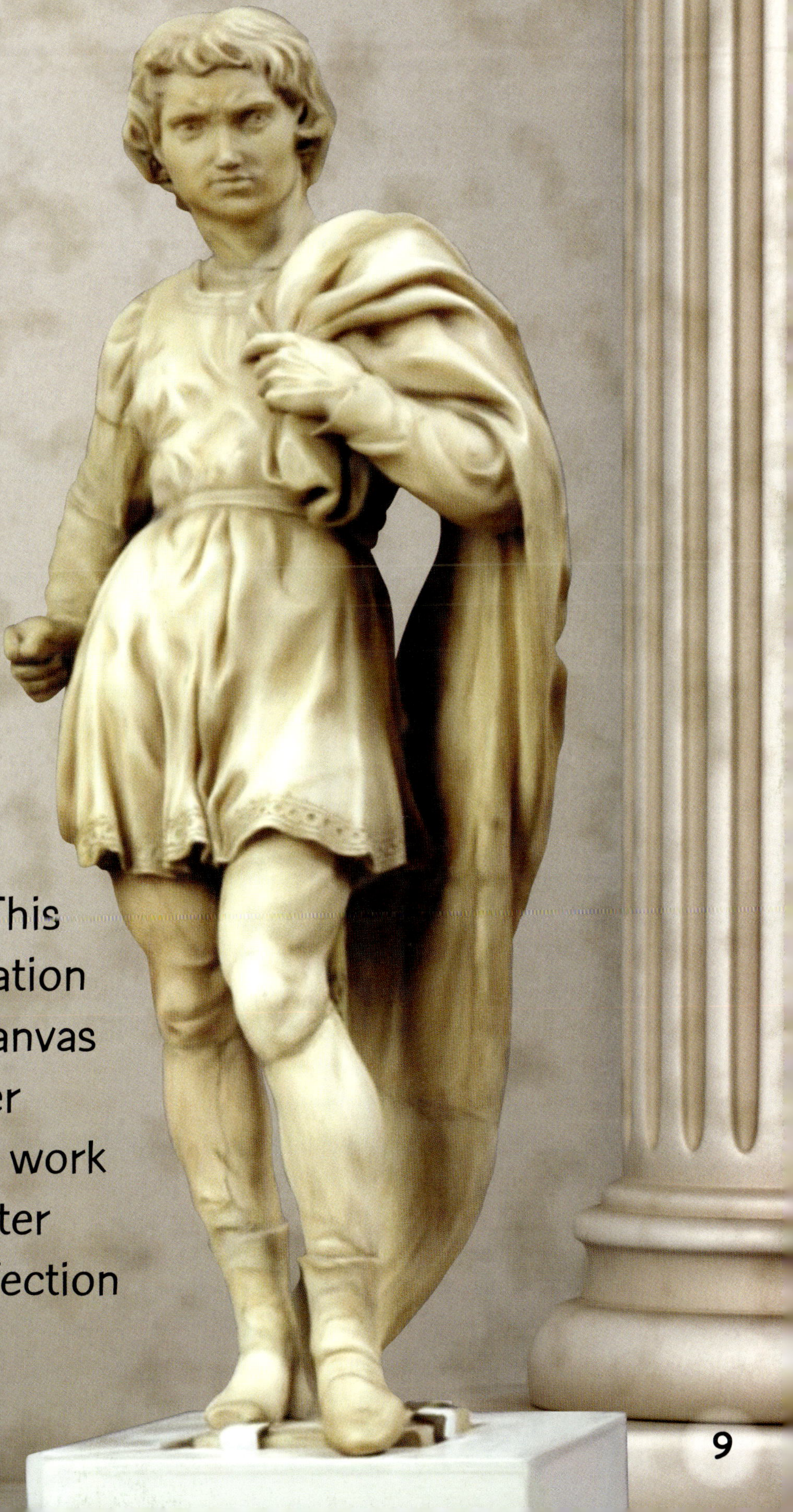

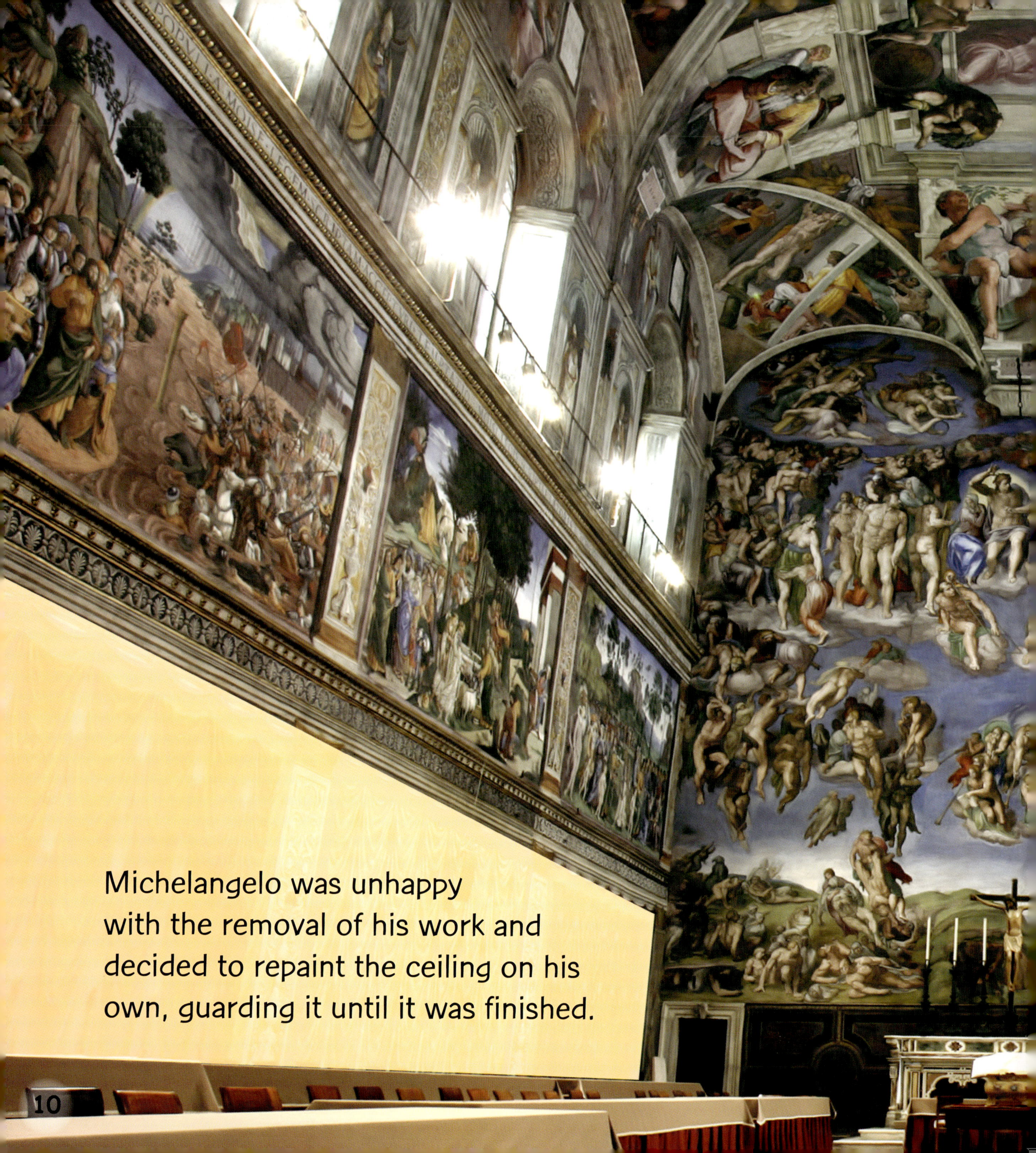

Michelangelo was unhappy with the removal of his work and decided to repaint the ceiling on his own, guarding it until it was finished.

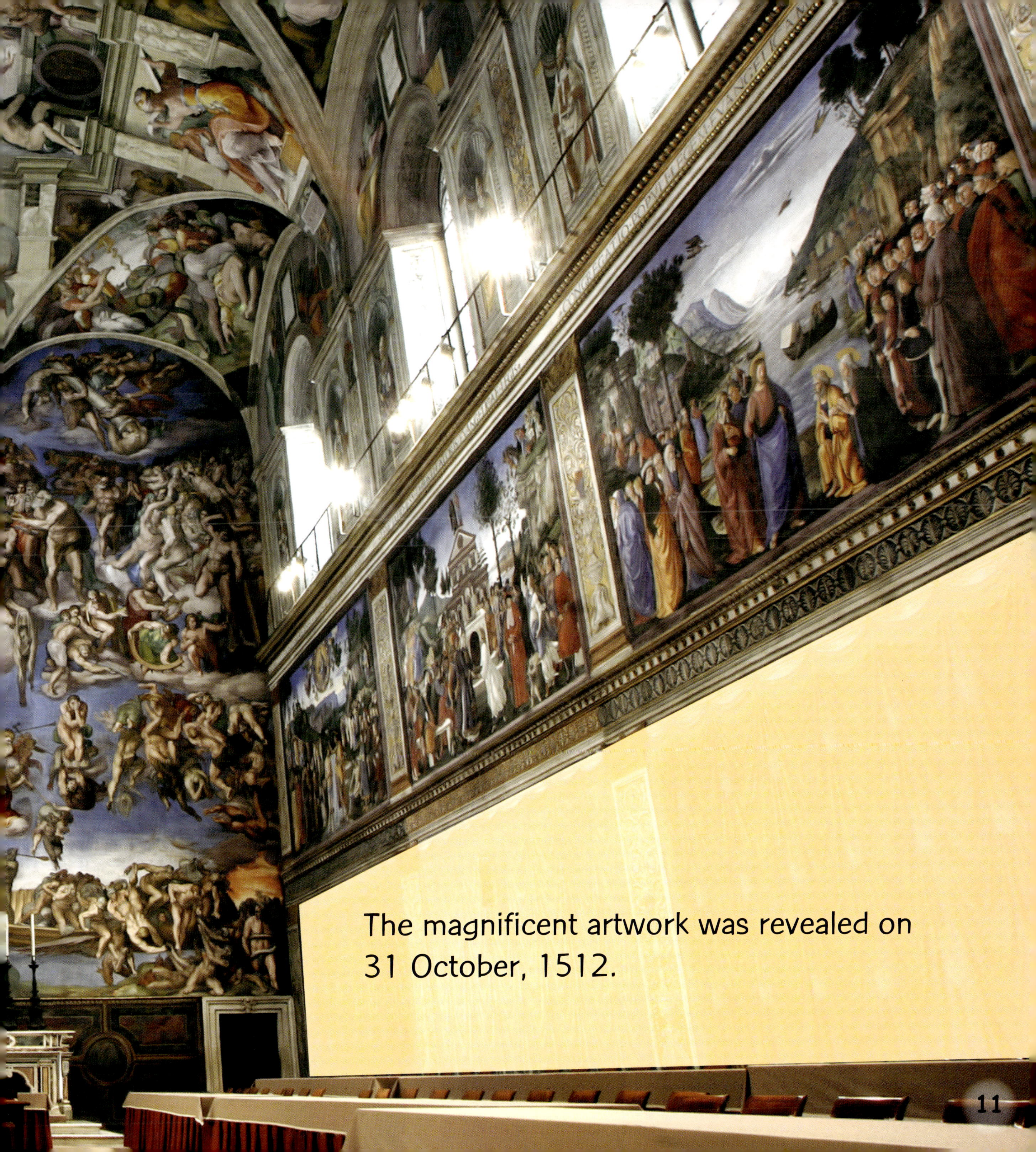

The magnificent artwork was revealed on 31 October, 1512.

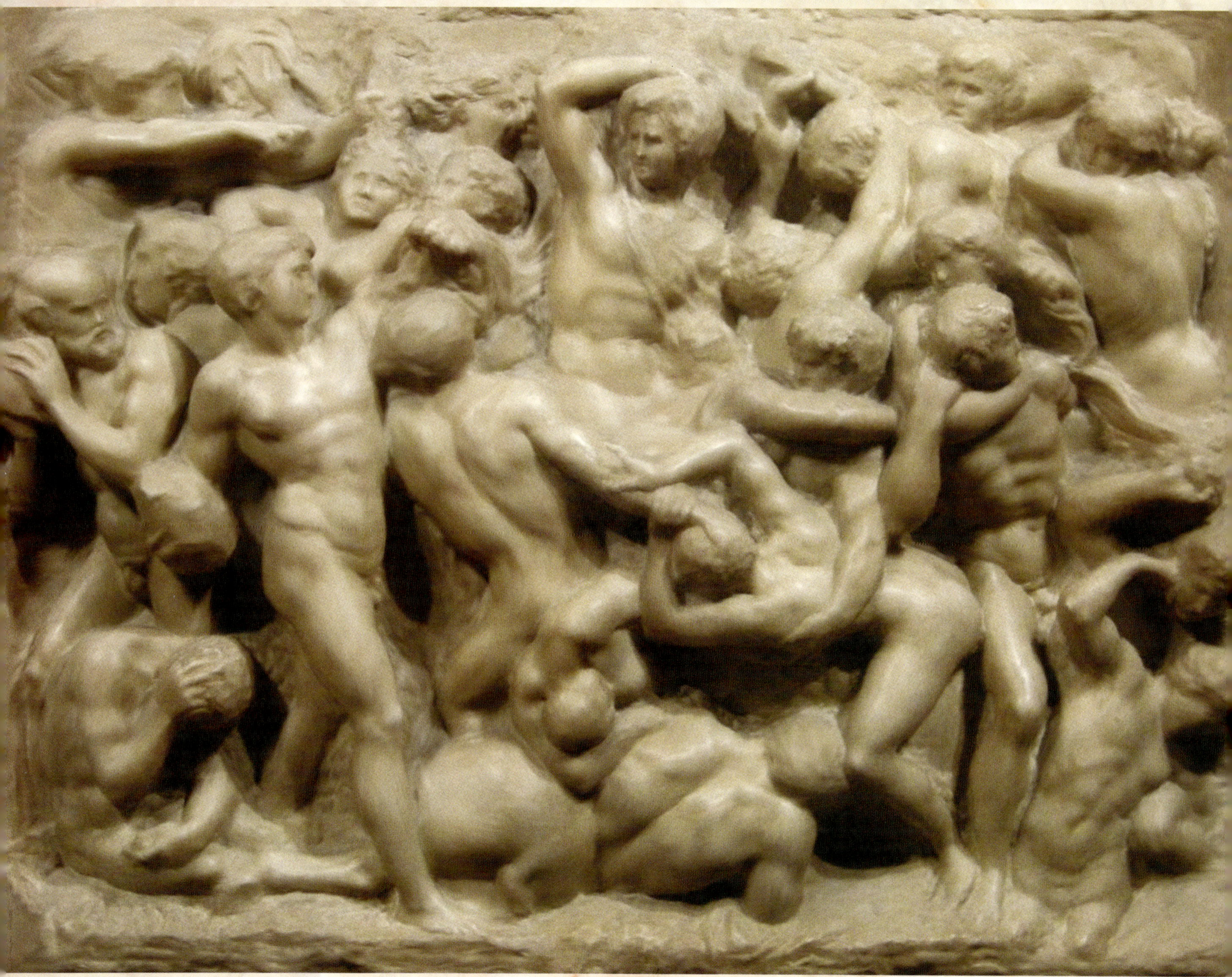

The strain of painting the Sistine Chapel took its toll on Michelangelo. While he continued to paint and sculpt, his primary focus was now on architecture.

Michelangelo designed some of the most prominent buildings of the time, including the Medici Chapel and the Laurentian Library (which housed the Medici book collection). The pinnacle of his success came when he was named chief architect of St. Peter's Basilica in 1546.

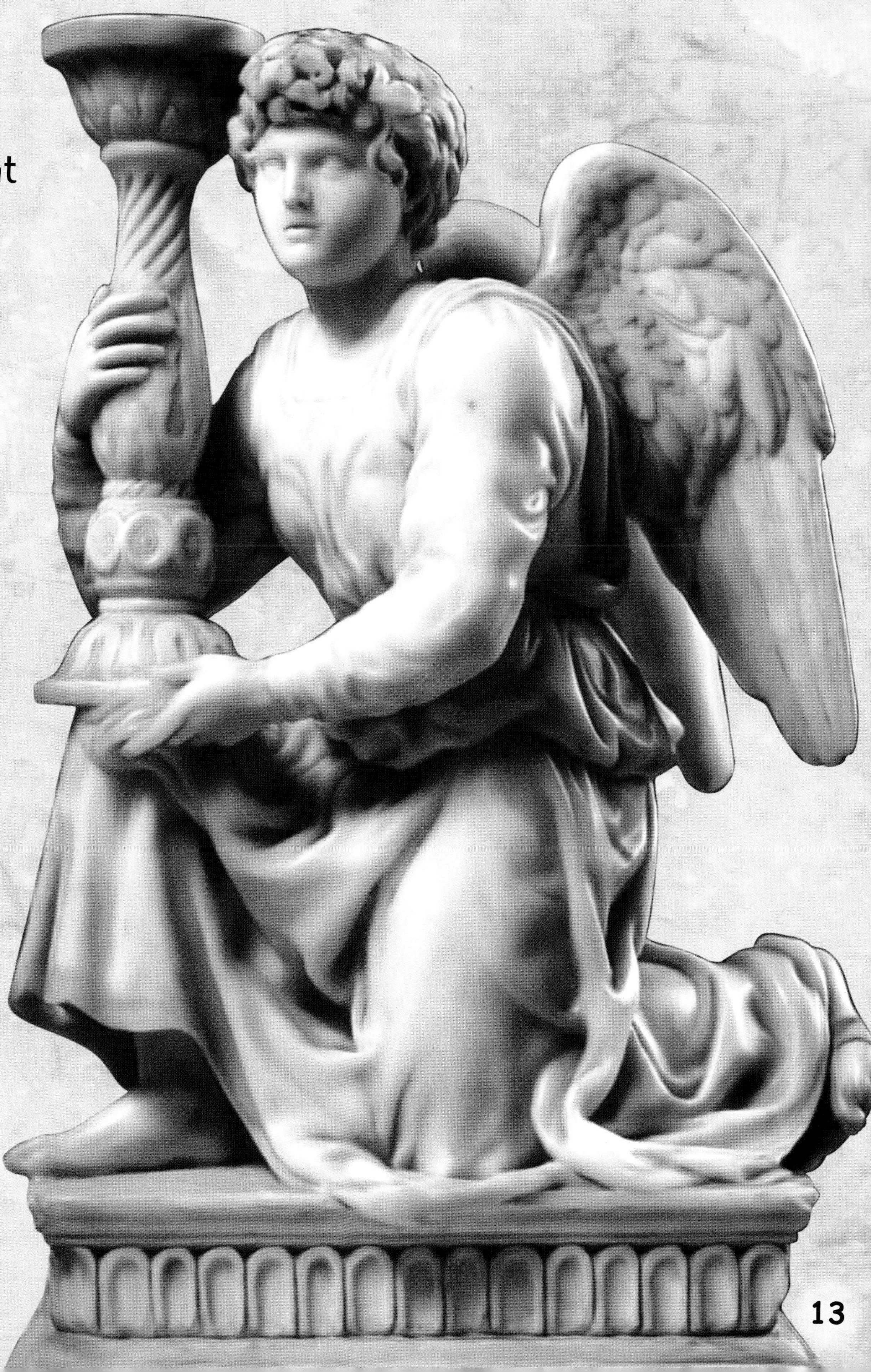

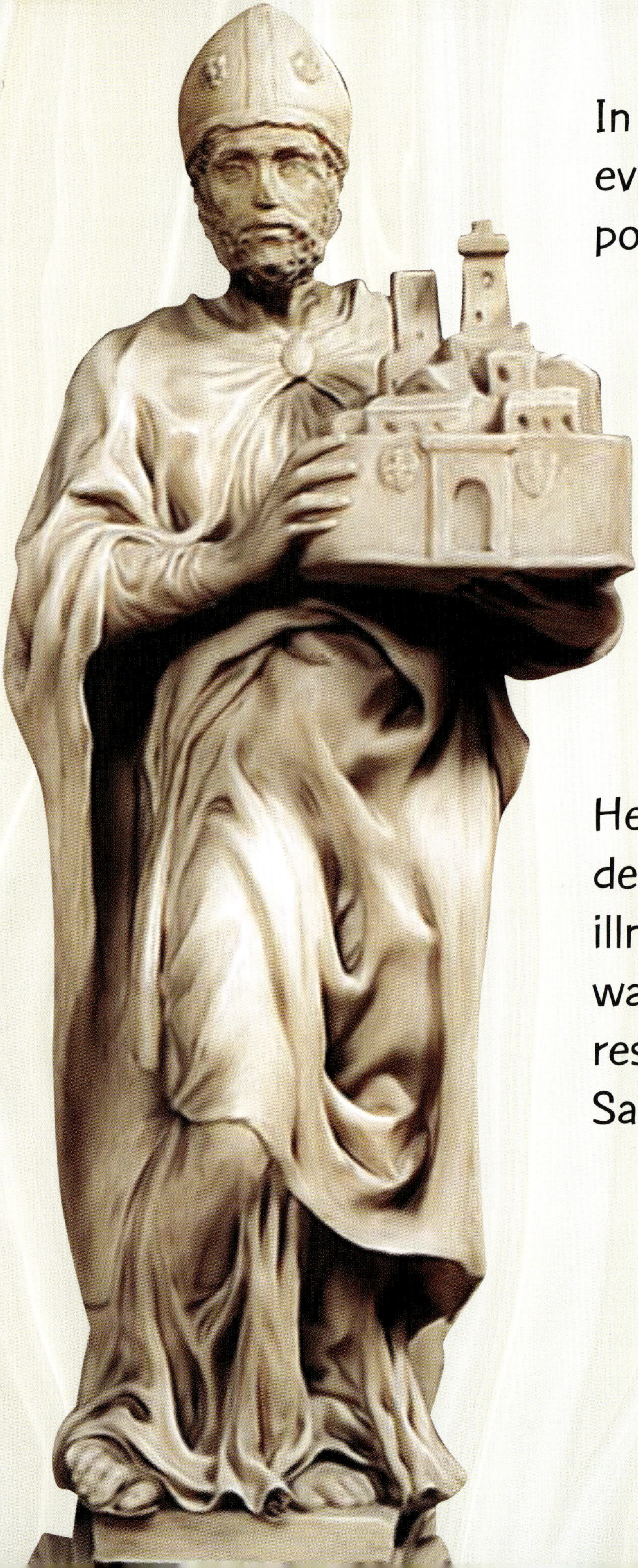

In his later years, Michelangelo even wrote hundreds of poems and sonnets.

He died in his house in Macel de' Corvi, Rome, after a brief illness at the age of 88. He was buried in his favoured resting place in Basilica di Santa Croce, Florence.

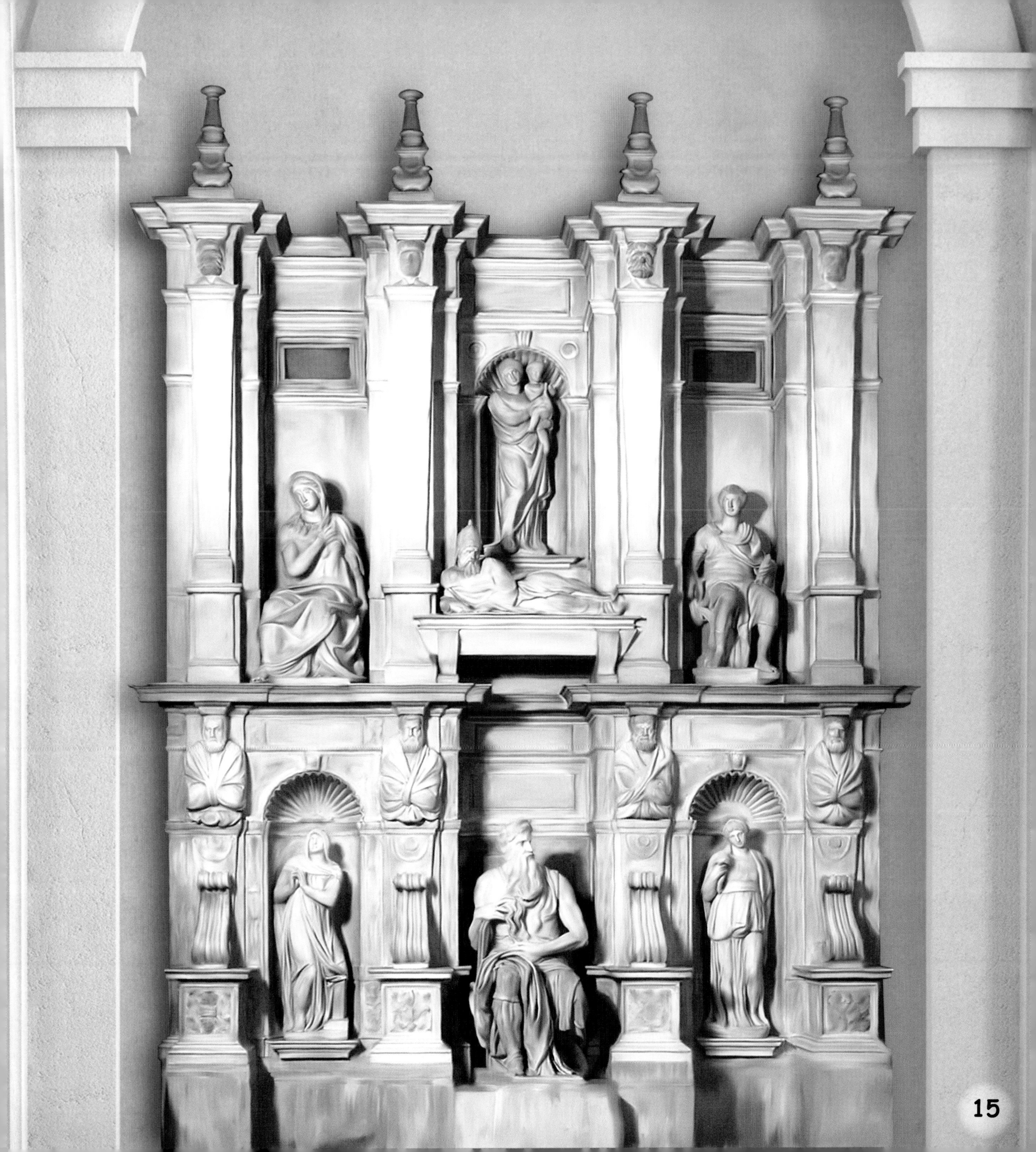

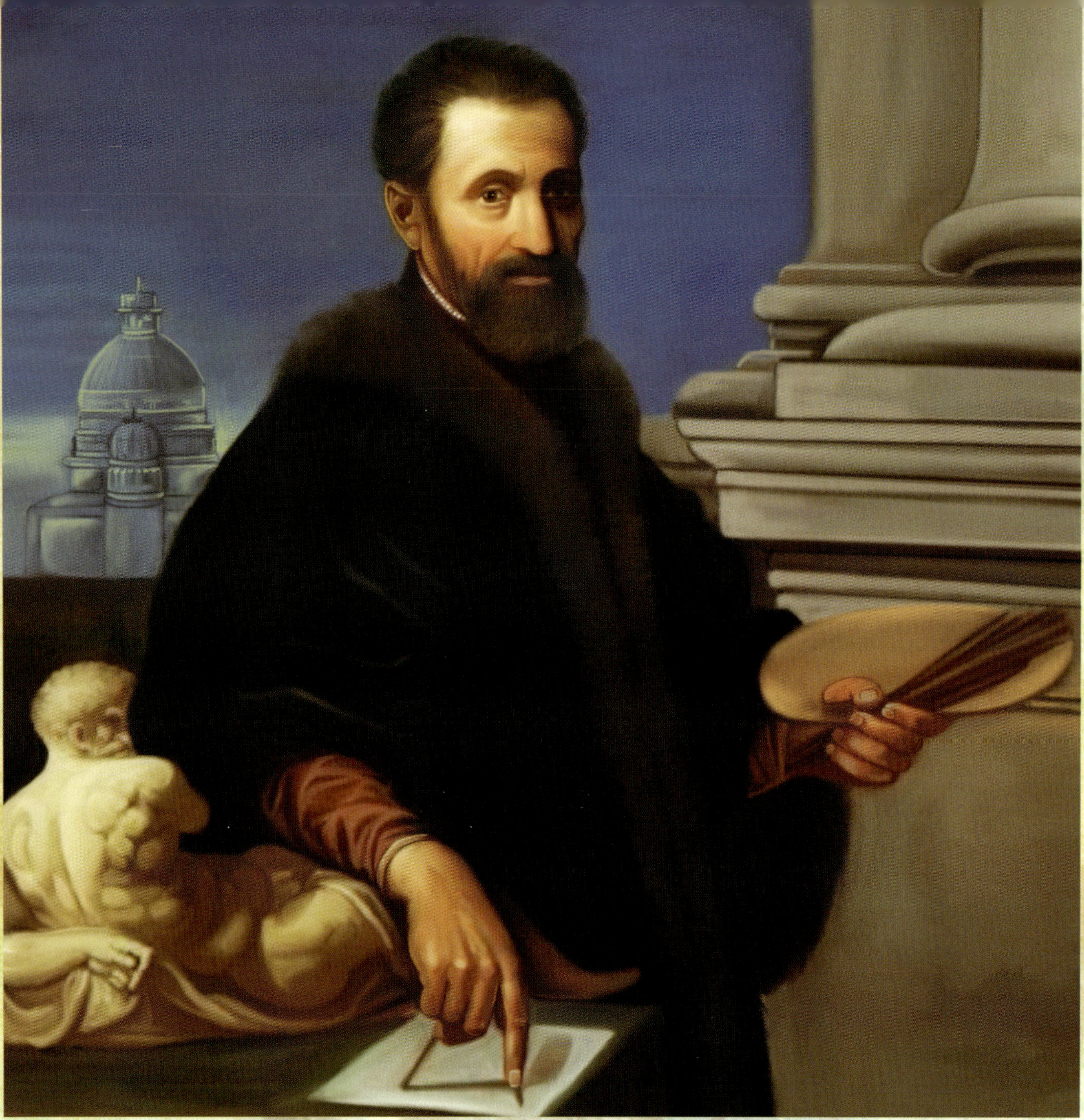

Unlike many artists, Michelangelo actually gained fame during his lifetime and was widely celebrated as 'Father and Master of All the Arts' by the public.

Art lovers from all over the world still head to Rome to view his work in the Sistine Chapel and to Florence to marvel at the sculpture of *David.*